ANDREW POLLAN

# Invisible Impact Anonymous Influence

*Anonymous Influence Profit Without Being Seen*

Copyright © 2024 by Andrew Pollan

All rights reserved. No part of this publication may be reproduced, stored or transmitted in any form or by any means, electronic, mechanical, photocopying, recording, scanning, or otherwise without written permission from the publisher. It is illegal to copy this book, post it to a website, or distribute it by any other means without permission.

First edition

This book was professionally typeset on Reedsy.
Find out more at reedsy.com

# Contents

| | |
|---|---|
| The Concept of FacelessMarketing | 1 |
| Establishing a Robust Online Presence | 5 |
| Developing Distinct Anonymous Brand Identities | 9 |
| Creating Engaging Content While Staying Anonymous | 13 |
| Harnessing Social Media for Anonymous Branding | 18 |
| Optimizing for Search Engines Without Personal Branding | 23 |
| Implementing Email Marketing with Anonymity | 28 |
| Revenue Generation Strategies for Faceless Brands | 33 |
| Measuring Success Through Analytics and Tracking | 40 |
| Final Thoughts and Future Trends | 45 |

# The Concept of FacelessMarketing

In today's digital world, personal branding is often highlighted as a vital ingredient for success. However, faceless marketing presents a strong alternative, enabling individuals and businesses to flourish without disclosing their personal identities. This guide explores the concept of faceless marketing, its core principles, benefits, and practical steps for those new to the approach.

**What is Faceless Marketing?**

Faceless marketing encompasses strategies and techniques that promote products, services, or content without linking them to a personal identity. Rather than centering a brand around a recognizable figure, this approach utilizes logos, themes, distinctive selling points, and consistent messaging to establish a memorable brand presence. It effectively maintains privacy, safeguards personal lives from public scrutiny, and directs focus toward the brand rather than the individual behind it.

**The Rise of Faceless Marketing**

The internet has made it easier for anyone to share content, launch a business, or become an influencer. However, this accessibility also brings challenges such as privacy concerns, identity theft, and blurred lines between personal and professional lives. Faceless marketing confronts these issues by allowing creators to retain anonymity while still engaging with their target audience.

## Benefits of Faceless Marketing

**Privacy and Security**: A key benefit of faceless marketing is the ability to keep personal identities private. This protects against risks like identity theft, harassment, or unwanted attention.

**Focus on Content and Quality**: This approach shifts emphasis from the individual to the content or product itself. It encourages creators to prioritize the quality and value of their offerings, resulting in a more authentic and customer-centered brand.

**Broad Appeal**: Faceless brands can attract a wider audience since they avoid biases associated with specific individuals. This inclusivity often leads to a more diverse and engaged following.

**Professional and Personal Separation**: Many individuals find it important to keep their personal and professional lives distinct. Faceless marketing allows for the development of successful careers or businesses online without compromising personal privacy.

**Scalability**: Faceless brands typically experience easier scalability and growth. Since the brand identity isn't tied to one person's image, it can adapt and expand without the constraints of personal branding.

## Examples of Successful Faceless Brands

Several brands have successfully utilized faceless marketing. For example, the popular blog "Wait But Why" engages millions with thought-provoking articles and illustrations while its author, Tim Urban, maintains relative anonymity. Similarly, the YouTube channel

"Kurzgesagt – In a Nutshell" produces high-quality educational content without focusing on individual creators, thus allowing the brand's unique style to shine.

**Getting Started with Faceless Marketing**

Define Your Brand Identity: Clearly articulate what your brand represents. Identify your values, mission, vision, and what differentiates you from competitors. This foundational understanding will inform all your marketing efforts.

**Create a Memorable Logo and Design**: A strong visual identity is crucial. Invest time in crafting an eye-catching logo and cohesive design elements that reflect your brand's personality and values. Consistency in visuals aids in building recognition.

**Craft Compelling Content**: Prioritize producing high-quality content that adds value to your audience. Whether through blog posts, videos, podcasts, or social media updates, ensure your content is informative and aligned with your brand's voice.

**Leverage Social Media**: Utilize social media platforms to share content, interact with followers, and foster a robust online presence. Ensure a uniform tone and style across every platform.

**Optimize for SEO**: Search engine optimization is essential for increasing your brand's online visibility. Conduct keyword research to understand what your target audience is searching for and incorporate these keywords into your content to attract organic traffic.

**Build an Email List**: Email marketing is an effective way to nurture relationships with your audience. Offer valuable content or incentives for email sign-ups, and use newsletters to keep your audience engaged.

**Analyze and Adapt**: Regularly assess your marketing efforts to identify what works and what doesn't. Use analytics tools to track key performance indicators (KPIs) like website traffic and engagement rates. Adjust your strategies using this data for optimal results.

## Challenges and Considerations

While faceless marketing has many advantages, it also poses challenges. Establishing trust and credibility can be harder without a personal face representing the brand. It's crucial to build trust through transparency, consistent quality, and excellent customer service. Balancing anonymity with the need for personalization in marketing can also be complex; finding ways to connect with your audience on a human level while maintaining privacy is essential for successful faceless marketing.

# Establishing a Robust Online Presence

A strong digital presence is essential for any faceless brand aiming to make an impact, attract an audience, and drive online revenue. This chapter provides a comprehensive guide to creating and optimizing your online platforms for maximum effect.

**Importance of a Professional Website and Branding**
- Your Website as Your Identity: The website serves as the primary touchpoint for potential customers, where they learn about your brand and offerings.
- Brand Recognition: A professional website and consistent branding help establish credibility and trust with your audience.

**Understanding Your Audience**
Before building your digital presence, it's vital to understand who your target audience is.

**Key Analyses:**

1. **Demographic Analysis**: Identify age, gender, location, and income level using tools like Google Analytics.
2. **Psychographic Analysis**: Understand lifestyle, interests, values, and attitudes through surveys and social media monitoring.

3. **Behavioral Analysis**: Observe interactions with your content and analyze online habits and preferences.

## Strategies for Creating a Recognizable Online Identity

### Creating a Professional Website

1. **Choose the Right Platform**: Select a website-building platform that aligns with your needs (e.g., WordPress, Wix, Squarespace).
2. **Design for User Experience (UX)**: Focus on easy navigation and a responsive design.
3. **Optimize for Speed and Performance**: Improve site speed by compressing images and using reliable hosting services.
4. **Focus on SEO**: Implement search engine optimization best practices to enhance visibility.
5. **Create Compelling Content**: Provide informative and engaging content, including an "About" page and product descriptions.
6. **Ensure Security**: Protect your website with security measures like SSL certificates.

### Leveraging Social Media Platforms

1. **Choose the Right Platforms**: Focus on platforms that resonate with your target audience (e.g., Facebook, Instagram).
2. **Create a Content Strategy**: Develop a plan that includes various content types and a consistent posting schedule.
3. **Engage with Your Audience**: Foster two-way communication by responding promptly to comments and questions.
4. **Utilize Hashtags and Keywords**: Increase post discoverability through relevant hashtags.
5. **Monitor and Analyze Performance**: Use analytics tools to track engagement and refine your social media strategy.
6. **Collaborate with Influencers and Partners**: Work with

influencers who align with your brand to expand reach.

**Building an Email List**

1. **Offer Valuable Incentives**: Encourage sign-ups with exclusive content or discounts.

2. **Segment Your Audience**: Tailor content for different audience segments to increase engagement.

3. **Craft Engaging Emails**: Write informative emails with compelling subject lines and clear calls to action.

4. **Automate Your Campaigns**: Use automation tools for welcome sequences and targeted emails.

5. **Analyze and Optimize**: Track metrics to improve email campaigns continuously.

**Leveraging SEO for Increased Visibility**

1. **Conduct Keyword Research**: Identify valuable keywords using tools like Google Keyword Planner.

2. **Optimize On-Page Elements**: Incorporate keywords into meta tags, headers, and URLs.

3. **Create High-Quality Content**: Regularly publish engaging content that addresses audience needs.

4. **Build Backlinks**: Acquire high-quality backlinks to boost site authority.

5. **Improve User Experience**: Ensure a positive user experience through fast loading times and easy navigation.

**Conclusion**

Building a robust online presence requires understanding your audience, creating a professional website, leveraging social media, cultivating an email list, and optimizing your content for search engines. By following these strategies, you can establish a strong digital identity that resonates with your audience and drives engagement.

# Developing Distinct Anonymous Brand Identities

In today's competitive market, creating a unique brand identity without relying on a personal face is essential. This chapter will provide strategies to develop a compelling anonymous brand identity that is memorable and resonates with your target audience.

**Understanding Brand Identity**

Brand identity consists of all the visual and verbal elements that represent your brand and set it apart from competitors. These elements include:

**Logo**: The key visual representation of your brand identity.
**Color Scheme**: The collection of colors that embodies your brand's character.
**Typography**: Fonts that convey your brand's voice.
**Tone of Voice**: The style of communication used in messaging.

When these elements are carefully integrated, they create a cohesive image that communicates your brand's values effectively.

**Defining Your Brand's Core Values**

Before developing visual elements, clarify your brand's core values. These values serve as the foundation for your identity and influence every aspect of your brand.

**Identify Your Mission**: Clearly articulate what your brand stands for, the problems it solves, and its purpose.

**Determine Your Vision**: Outline your long-term aspirations and where you envision your brand heading.

**Establish Your Values**: Identify key principles that guide your decisions and behavior, such as integrity and innovation.

**Creating a Memorable Logo**

Your logo is often the first thing people associate with your brand, making it crucial for recognition.

**Simplicity and Versatility**: A straightforward design is easier to remember and should work well in various formats.

**Relevance and Meaning**: Ensure your logo reflects the essence of your brand through appropriate shapes, symbols, and colors.

**Timelessness**: Design a logo that remains effective over time, avoiding fleeting trends.

**Professional Design**: Consider hiring a designer to craft a logo that enhances your brand's perception.

Developing a Consistent Color Scheme

Colors evoke emotions and play a significant role in shaping perceptions of your brand.

**Color Psychology**: Select colors based on their emotional impact; for example, blue conveys trust, while red can create excitement.

**Consistency**: Maintain uniformity in color usage across all materials to strengthen brand recognition.

**Contrast and Balance**: Use contrasting colors thoughtfully to ensure readability and aesthetic appeal.

**Selecting Appropriate Typography**

Typography is another key component of brand identity, influencing how your message is received.

**Brand Personality**: Choose fonts that reflect the character of your brand, whether traditional or modern.

**Readability**: Prioritize legibility, especially in smaller sizes, avoiding overly ornate fonts.

**Consistency**: Limit font choices to two or three styles to maintain a unified appearance.

Crafting a Unique Tone of Voice

Your brand's tone of voice is vital for connecting with your audience.

**Define Your Brand's Personality**: Determine whether your tone is friendly, authoritative, casual, or formal.

**Consistency Across Channels**: Use the same tone in all communications to build trust and recognition.

**Adaptability**: While maintaining a foundational tone, adjust it to suit different contexts (e.g., more casual on social media).

Creating a Style Guide

A style guide serves as a reference for maintaining consistency in your brand identity.

**Visual Elements**: Outline guidelines for logo usage, colors, typography, and imagery.

Tone of Voice: Provide examples of how to express your tone in various contexts.

Brand Story: Share your mission, vision, and values to ensure everyone understands the brand's core principles.

**Application Examples**: Include real-world instances showcasing your brand identity in action.

Implementing and Evolving Your Brand Identity

Once your brand identity is established, it's crucial to implement it consistently across all platforms.

**Training and Onboarding**: Educate team members on the style guide and the importance of maintaining consistency.

**Regular Audits**: Periodically review materials to ensure alignment with your brand identity and make necessary adjustments.

**Adapt and Evolve**: Stay open to evolving your identity as market conditions change or as new insights emerge; update your style guide accordingly.

Crafting an effective anonymous brand identity involves strategic planning and consistent execution. By defining core values, creating compelling visual elements, and implementing a detailed style guide, you can establish a memorable brand that thrives in the competitive landscape of faceless marketing.

# Creating Engaging Content While Staying Anonymous

Creating captivating and high-quality content is essential for any effective marketing strategy, particularly in the realm of faceless marketing. This unique approach presents both challenges and opportunities. Since there is no personal identity to anchor the brand, your content must be even more engaging and strategically designed to foster trust, connect with your audience, and drive conversions. This chapter will provide you with a comprehensive guide to producing content that captivates and converts, all while maintaining your anonymity.

**The Importance of Content in Faceless Marketing**

Content acts as the voice of your brand, serving as the medium through which you communicate your message, share expertise, and connect with your audience. In faceless marketing, content assumes an even greater significance as it becomes the primary means through which your brand establishes its identity and cultivates relationships.

**Key Roles of Content**

**Building Trust and Authority**: High-quality content positions your brand as a credible and knowledgeable authority in your niche. By delivering valuable insights and solutions, you can cultivate trust and loyalty among your audience.

**Driving Engagement**: Engaging content stimulates interaction and fosters community. It can ignite conversations, solicit feedback, and create a dedicated following.

**Boosting SEO and Visibility**: Well-crafted, search engine-optimized content can substantially enhance your brand's online visibility. By targeting relevant keywords and producing valuable content, you can attract organic traffic and improve search engine rankings.

**Facilitating Conversions**: Effective content guides your audience through their buying journey—from awareness to consideration to decision-making—by addressing their needs and pain points at each stage, ultimately driving conversions and business growth.

## Types of Content Suitable for Faceless Marketing

A robust content strategy entails a diverse mix of content types tailored to your audience's preferences and your brand's strengths. Below are effective content types for faceless marketing:

**Blog Posts**: Blogging is an impactful way to share knowledge and attract organic traffic. Focus on creating informative, well-researched, SEO-optimized posts that address your audience's interests and challenges.

**Videos**: Video content is versatile and engaging. You can produce explainer videos, tutorials, product demonstrations, and animations without revealing your identity. Utilize captivating visuals, clear narration, and storytelling to engage viewers.

**Infographics**: Infographics present complex information in visually appealing formats that are easy to digest, making them ideal for conveying statistics or step-by-step processes.

**Podcasts**: Audio content such as podcasts provides an opportunity to share insights, interviews, and narratives without visual exposure. Podcasts are convenient for audiences on the move and can help position your brand as an authority.

**E-books and Guides**: Comprehensive long-form content like e-books and guides can delve deeply into specific topics. They also serve as excellent lead magnets for building email lists.

**Social Media Posts**: Social media platforms facilitate the sharing of bite-sized content and interaction with audiences. Use a blend of text, images, videos, and stories to keep followers engaged.

**Strategies for Creating Engaging Content**

To craft content that resonates with your audience, employ these strategic approaches:

**Understand Your Audience**: Conduct thorough research to grasp your target audience's demographics, interests, pain points, and preferences. This insight will help you create relevant content.

**Deliver Value**: Ensure your content informs, entertains, or addresses the challenges faced by your audience. By consistently delivering valuable insights, you can build trust and loyalty.

**Tell Stories**: Storytelling connects with audiences emotionally. Use narratives to illustrate points and share experiences that resonate with them.

**Use Visuals Effectively**: Enhance the appeal of your content by incorporating high-quality visuals, graphics, and videos that complement your written material.

**Maintain Consistency**: A consistent tone, style, and posting schedule help establish a strong brand identity.

**Optimize for SEO**: Implement SEO best practices by conducting keyword research and naturally incorporating relevant keywords into your content to improve visibility.

**Encourage Interaction**: Foster community by inviting comments and feedback from your audience. Respond promptly to inquiries to enhance engagement.

**Analyze and Adapt**: Regularly assess the performance of your content using analytics tools to track metrics like traffic and engagement. Leverage these insights to enhance your approach.

## Tools and Resources for Content Creation

**Leverage various tools to streamline the content creation process:**

Content Management Systems (CMS): Platforms like WordPress, Wix, and Squarespace simplify content creation and management.

**Graphic Design Tools**: Tools such as Canva, Adobe Spark, and Visme enable you to design infographics and social media graphics without advanced design skills.

**Video Editing Software**: Programs like Adobe Premiere Pro or simpler options like iMovie help create polished video content.

**Podcasting Tools**: Use tools like Audacity or Anchor for recording, editing, and distributing podcast episodes easily.

**SEO Tools**: Google Keyword Planner, Ahrefs, or SEMrush assist in keyword research and performance tracking.

**Content Planning Tools**: Organize your creation process with tools like Trello or Asana to keep your efforts on schedule.

## Overcoming Challenges in Faceless Content Creation

While faceless content creation offers distinct advantages, it also presents unique challenges:

**Building Trust**: To counter the absence of a personal face, focus on delivering consistent high-quality content that provides value and engages users.

**Creating Engaging Visuals**: Without personal visuals, invest in high-quality graphics and animations to make your content visually appealing.

**Maintaining Authenticity**: Convey authenticity through storytelling, transparent communication, and genuine audience engagement.

**Standing Out**: Differentiate your brand by emphasizing your unique value proposition along with consistent branding and high-quality content.

Creating engaging content while remaining anonymous is both an art and a science. By understanding your audience's needs, providing value, employing storytelling techniques, and utilizing the right tools, you can craft compelling content that drives engagement and conversions effectively. In subsequent chapters, we will explore additional strategies to enhance your faceless marketing efforts further.

# Harnessing Social Media for Anonymous Branding

Social media platforms have revolutionized marketing, providing a vital connection to millions of potential customers globally. For brands aiming to maintain anonymity, these platforms offer unique opportunities to establish a presence, engage audiences, and drive traffic while keeping personal identities concealed. This chapter delves into best practices for anonymous engagement on social media, strategies for cultivating a following without compromising privacy, and tailored content approaches for different channels.

## Best Practices for Anonymous Engagement on Social Platforms

### Selecting the Ideal Platforms

The foundation of a successful social media strategy lies in choosing the right platforms that align with your target audience and business objectives. Each platform has distinct characteristics and demographics:

**Facebook**: With approximately 2.8 billion monthly active users, Facebook is versatile and excels in community building and broad audience engagement.

**Instagram**: This visually-driven platform is perfect for brands with strong imagery, appealing mainly to younger demographics and industries like fashion, beauty, and lifestyle.

**Twitter**: Ideal for real-time updates and customer interaction, Twitter facilitates quick and engaging conversations around trending topics.

**LinkedIn**: As a professional networking site, LinkedIn is suited for B2B marketing, thought leadership, and connecting with industry professionals.

**YouTube**: The second-largest search engine, YouTube is powerful for video content, making it perfect for tutorials and educational material.

**Pinterest**: A visual discovery engine that effectively drives website traffic, particularly in niches such as home decor, fashion, and DIY.

## Establishing a Consistent Brand Identity

Creating a recognizable and trustworthy brand on social media requires consistency, even in anonymity. Key elements include:

**Visual Cohesion**: Maintain a consistent color palette, logo, and design across all profiles to enhance brand recognition.

**Unified Tone**: Develop a clear tone of voice that reflects your brand's personality—be it friendly, professional, or humorous—and use it consistently in communications.

**Content Themes**: Identify core content themes that resonate with your brand values and audience interests (e.g., a fitness brand focusing on workout tips and nutrition advice).

## Content Strategies Tailored for Different Social Media Channels

### Crafting Compelling Content

Compelling content is essential for capturing and keeping your audience's attention. Strategies for creating impactful content include:

**High-Quality Visuals**: Utilize tools like Canva or Adobe Spark to produce appealing images, graphics, and videos that resonate with your audience.

**Storytelling**: Share narratives that emotionally connect with your audience—be it customer success stories or insights into your brand values.

**Interactive Elements**: Foster engagement through polls, quizzes, and Q&A sessions, which not only engages but also provides insights into audience preferences.

**Educational Content**: Offer valuable information that addresses audience pain points—such as how-to guides or industry insights.

**User-Generated Content**: Encourage followers to share their experiences and feature their content to foster community trust.

### Engaging Your Audience

Building relationships through active engagement is vital for creating a sense of community:

**Timely Responses**: Respond promptly to comments and messages to show appreciation for audience interaction.

**Encouraging Dialogue**: Pose open-ended questions to invite conversation and deepen engagement.

**Acknowledging Contributions:** Show gratitude by interacting with followers' content through likes and shares.

**Handling Feedback**: Address criticism constructively to demonstrate openness to improvement.

### Utilizing Hashtags and Keywords

Incorporating hashtags and keywords can enhance the visibility of your content:

**Relevant Hashtags**: Use trending hashtags to broaden your reach; tools like Hashtagify can assist in identifying effective options.

**Branded Hashtags**: Create a unique branded hashtag to encourage user-generated content and track brand mentions.

**Keyword Inclusion**: Optimize your profiles and posts with relevant keywords to improve search visibility.

## Analyzing Performance and Adapting Strategies

Regular performance analysis informs strategy refinement:

**Platform Analytics**: Utilize built-in analytics tools to monitor metrics such as engagement rates and follower growth.

**Third-Party Tools**: Consider tools like Hootsuite or Buffer for comprehensive analytics across multiple platforms.

**A/B Testing**: Experiment with various content types and posting times to identify what resonates most with your audience.

**Feedback Incorporation**: Analyze audience feedback alongside performance data to identify trends and opportunities for improvement.

## Collaborating with Influencers and Partners

Strategic partnerships can amplify reach and credibility:

**Identifying Influencers**: Seek influencers within your niche who resonate with your target audience; tools like BuzzSumo can aid in this process.

**Building Relationships**: Focus on authentic collaborations with influencers who genuinely align with your brand values.

**Co-Creating Content**: Develop collaborative initiatives such as webinars or giveaways to leverage mutual strengths.

**Measuring Collaboration Impact**: Track the effectiveness of partnerships through metrics like engagement rates and traffic increases.

Social media serves as a powerful avenue for anonymous branding, presenting numerous opportunities to build a reputation, engage audiences, and drive growth. By selecting appropriate platforms, crafting compelling content, fostering genuine engagement, and leveraging analytics, brands can achieve success while maintaining anonymity in their marketing efforts.

# Optimizing for Search Engines Without Personal Branding

**Introduction to SEO for Faceless Websites**

In today's digital marketplace, search engine optimization (SEO) is vital for enhancing online visibility and driving organic traffic. For brands operating without a personal touch, mastering SEO is crucial to achieving recognition and success without relying on individual identities. This chapter will explore essential strategies and techniques for optimizing faceless websites while maintaining anonymity.

**Understanding SEO Fundamentals**

SEO consists of various practices aimed at improving a website's ranking in search engine results pages (SERPs). By enhancing your website's visibility, you can attract more organic visitors. Key components of SEO include:

**Keyword Research**: The foundation of effective SEO lies in identifying the right keywords that potential customers use in their searches.

**On-Page SEO**: This focuses on optimizing individual web pages to enhance relevance and traffic.

**Technical SEO**: Ensures that the backend of your website meets the technical standards set by search engines.

**Link Building**: Acquiring backlinks from reputable sites to establish authority and trustworthiness.

## Keyword Research for Faceless Brands

Conducting thorough keyword research is essential for effectively targeting your audience. Here are steps to guide your keyword research:

**Identify Core Topics**: Recognize broad themes relevant to your business; for example, "sustainable living" for eco-friendly product stores.

**Utilize Keyword Tools**: Leverage platforms like Google Keyword Planner, Ahrefs, and SEMrush to discover relevant keywords based on search volume and difficulty.

**Competitor Analysis**: Examine the keywords your competitors rank for to identify opportunities and gaps in your strategy.

**Focus on Long-Tail Keywords**: Target longer, specific phrases that may have lower search volumes but higher conversion potential.

**Understand User Intent**: Tailor content to address the specific needs of users based on their search intent.

## Best Practices for On-Page SEO

Optimizing individual pages is critical for improved search rankings. Key on-page SEO practices include:

**Title Tags**: Craft unique, keyword-rich title tags under 60 characters for each page to ensure full visibility in search results.

**Meta Descriptions**: Write engaging meta descriptions that summarize content and include target keywords to boost click-through rates.

**Headers (H1, H2, H3)**: Use header tags to structure content effectively, ensuring the main keyword appears in the H1 tag.

**Strategic Keyword Use**: Seamlessly incorporate keywords within the content, ensuring natural flow and avoiding overuse.

**Internal Linking**: Connect related pages within your site to help search engines understand your site's structure and improve linked pages' rankings.

**Image Optimization**: Optimize images with descriptive filenames and alt text containing relevant keywords for better visibility in image searches.

## Essential Aspects of Technical SEO

Technical SEO ensures compliance with search engines' technical requirements, focusing on:

**Site Speed**: Optimize loading times to enhance user experience and improve rankings using tools like Google PageSpeed Insights.

**Mobile-Friendliness**: Implement responsive design to accommodate mobile users, who represent a significant portion of web traffic.

Secure Connections (HTTPS): Use HTTPS to secure your site, enhancing trust and compliance with ranking factors.

**XML Sitemap**: Create an XML sitemap for efficient indexing by search engines.

**Robots.txt**: Utilize a robots.txt file to manage crawler access, directing them on which pages to crawl.

## Strategies for Building High-Quality Backlinks

Acquiring backlinks from authoritative sites signals content value to search engines. Consider these strategies:

**Guest Blogging**: Contribute guest posts to respected blogs within your niche, including links back to your site.

**Content Marketing**: Develop shareable content such as infographics or comprehensive guides that naturally attract backlinks.

**Outreach Efforts**: Connect with bloggers, influencers, and journalists to share valuable content resources.

**Broken Link Building**: Identify broken links on other websites and propose your content as a replacement.

**Directories and Listings**: Submit your website to reputable directories and industry-specific listings for enhanced visibility and backlinks.

## Monitoring and Measuring SEO Performance

Regularly assessing SEO performance is vital for understanding effectiveness. Use these tools and metrics:

**Google Analytics**: Monitor organic traffic, user behavior, and conversion rates to identify successful pages and areas needing improvement.

**Google Search Console**: Track keyword rankings, click-through rates, and indexing issues to evaluate site presence in search results.

**SEO Tools**: Utilize platforms like Ahrefs, SEMrush, or Moz for in-depth analysis of keyword rankings and site audits.

**Focus Metrics**: Pay attention to organic traffic, bounce rates, average session durations, and conversion rates as indicators of user engagement.

## Maintaining Anonymity in SEO Practices

Achieving effective SEO while preserving anonymity requires strategic approaches:

**Brand Emphasis**: Center your marketing efforts around your brand name and mission instead of individual identities.

**Content Quality**: Deliver high-quality content that fulfills audience needs to organically attract traffic and backlinks.

**Authentic Engagement**: Interact with your audience using a consistent brand voice without revealing personal information.

**Anonymous Author Profiles**: Utilize brand personas or collective author profiles to maintain anonymity while establishing credibility.

By effectively leveraging SEO techniques, faceless brands can significantly boost online visibility and attract targeted audiences without sacrificing anonymity. Comprehensive keyword research, meticulous on-page optimization, robust technical SEO practices, and strategic link-building efforts are essential for achieving high search rankings and driving organic traffic while remaining faceless.

# Implementing Email Marketing with Anonymity

Email marketing is a cornerstone of digital marketing strategy, providing direct access to your audience and delivering impressive returns on investment. For marketers seeking to maintain anonymity, email marketing offers a distinctive avenue to cultivate relationships, engage leads, and drive conversions without disclosing personal identities. This chapter delves into effective strategies for executing email marketing campaigns while preserving anonymity.

**The Significance of Email Marketing**

Email marketing excels in its ability to personalize communication, delivering tailored content straight to subscribers' inboxes. This is particularly advantageous for faceless marketing, as the focus shifts to content quality rather than individual personalities.

**Key Benefits**:

**Direct Communication**: Email serves as a straightforward channel to connect with your audience, cutting through the noise of social media and search engines.

**Personalization**: Utilize tools that allow customization of emails to meet the specific needs and preferences of subscribers.

**Automation**: Leverage automation features in email platforms to nurture leads and sustain engagement with minimal effort.

**Measurable Results**: Email marketing is easily trackable, enabling you to assess open rates, click-through rates, conversions, and other key metrics.

## Building an Email List

A robust email list is foundational to a successful email marketing strategy. Below are strategies for effectively growing your list while maintaining anonymity:

**Strategies for List Building**:

**Opt-In Forms**: Incorporate opt-in forms across your website, blog, and social media profiles. Offer attractive incentives like e-books or exclusive content to encourage sign-ups.

**Lead Magnets**: Develop compelling lead magnets that deliver immediate value, such as free guides or discount codes relevant to your audience's interests.

**Landing Pages**: Create dedicated landing pages focused on email sign-ups, ensuring a clear value proposition and persuasive call-to-action.

**Pop-Ups and Slide-Ins**: Use pop-ups and slide-ins judiciously to capture email addresses. When well-designed and used sparingly, they can be effective.

**Social Media Promotion**: Utilize social media platforms to promote your email list through posts, stories, and targeted ads.

## Crafting Engaging Email Content

The effectiveness of your emails hinges on their content. Here's how to create compelling emails while remaining faceless:

**Content Creation Tips:**

**Welcome Emails:** The initial email should warmly welcome subscribers, introduce your brand, explain what they can expect, and deliver promised lead magnets.

**Educational Content:** Share valuable educational materials such as how-to guides, industry insights, and relevant news tailored to your audience's interests.

**Promotional Emails:** While not every communication should be promotional, don't hesitate to share details about special offers or new products.

**Personalization Techniques:** Enhance relevance by personalizing emails with subscribers' first names and tailoring content based on their preferences.

**Storytelling:** Engage recipients through storytelling by sharing customer success stories or narratives that align with your brand's mission.

**Clear Calls to Action (CTA):** Each email should include a clear and compelling CTA, guiding subscribers towards desired actions like reading a blog or making a purchase.

### Designing Effective Emails

Email design significantly affects engagement levels. Aim for visually appealing and user-friendly designs.

**Design Best Practices:**

**Responsive Design:** Ensure emails are optimized for all devices, especially mobile phones and tablets.

**Clean Layouts:** Adopt a simple layout that emphasizes key messages while avoiding clutter.

**Visual Elements:** Use relevant visuals like images and infographics to enhance engagement while ensuring they are optimized for quick loading.

**Consistent Branding**: Maintain consistent branding elements such as colors and logos across all communications for brand recognition.

**Accessibility Considerations**: Design with accessibility in mind by using readable fonts and providing alt text for images.

## Automation and Segmentation

Automation and segmentation are powerful strategies that enhance email marketing impact by ensuring targeted messaging.

**Automation Techniques**:

**Automated Sequences**: Implement automated email sequences for lead nurturing and subscriber engagement, including welcome series and re-engagement campaigns.

**Behavioral Triggers**: Send personalized emails triggered by specific subscriber actions, such as resource downloads or cart abandonments.

**Segmentation Strategies**: Segment your email list based on demographics or behavior for more targeted messaging.

**A/B Testing**: Conduct A/B tests on subject lines, content, and design elements to identify what resonates best with your audience.

## Analyzing and Optimizing Performance

Regular analysis is vital for refining your email marketing strategy. Utilize these metrics for performance tracking:

**Metrics to Monitor**:

**Open Rates**: Assess open rates to gauge the effectiveness of subject lines and overall email appeal.

**Click-Through Rates (CTR)**: Monitor CTR to evaluate content engagement and CTA effectiveness.

**Conversion Rates**: Analyze conversion rates to measure how many subscribers complete desired actions.

**Bounce Rates**: Track bounce rates to maintain sender reputation and ensure deliverability.

**Unsubscribe Rates**: Keep an eye on unsubscribe rates as high rates may indicate content misalignment with subscriber expectations.

**Analytics Tools**: Utilize platforms like Mailchimp or ActiveCampaign for detailed analytics and reporting insights.

## Maintaining Anonymity in Email Marketing

Safeguarding anonymity in email marketing requires strategic planning:

**Anonymity Strategies**:

**Brand-Centric Focus**: Center communications around the brand rather than individuals, using a consistent brand name and logo.

**Generic Email Addresses**: Employ generic email addresses (e.g., info@yourbrand.com) instead of personal names to maintain anonymity.

**Transparent Communication**: Clearly communicate the rationale behind collecting email addresses and how they will be used, providing options for managing preferences or unsubscribing.

**Professional Sign-Offs**: Use professional sign-offs that reflect the brand identity (e.g., "The [Brand Name] Team") instead of individual names.

Email marketing serves as a potent tool for faceless brands, facilitating direct engagement with audiences while preserving anonymity. By focusing on building robust email lists, crafting engaging content, optimizing designs, automating processes, and continuously analyzing performance, you can achieve substantial results without revealing personal identities. Subsequent chapters will delve into advanced techniques to further enhance your faceless marketing strategies.

# Revenue Generation Strategies for Faceless Brands

Establishing a faceless brand can be a remarkable accomplishment, but the true challenge lies in transforming that brand into a sustainable source of income. This chapter delves into diverse monetization strategies tailored for anonymous ventures, emphasizing methods that allow you to maintain your privacy. From digital products to affiliate marketing, these approaches will enable you to generate revenue while safeguarding your identity.

**Developing and Marketing Digital Products**

One of the most powerful ways to monetize a faceless brand is through the creation and sale of digital products. These offerings are generally low-cost to produce and can scale significantly.

**1. E-Books and Comprehensive Guides**

Create informative e-books or detailed guides that encapsulate your expertise. You can sell these directly on your website or utilize platforms such as Amazon Kindle. Ensure that your material is both informative and meticulously researched to attract potential buyers.

**2. Online Learning Programs**

Design and market online courses that instruct users on specific skills or topics within your niche. Platforms like Udemy, Teachable, and Thinkific facilitate easy hosting and selling of your courses. Incorporate engaging video materials, downloadable resources, and interactive features to enrich the learning experience.

### 3. Software Solutions and Applications

If you possess technical skills, think about developing software applications or tools that address particular challenges or needs in your industry. This could range from productivity applications to specialized software aimed at niche markets.

### 4. Subscription-Based Membership Websites

Provide exclusive content, tools, and community engagement through a membership site. Charge a recurring fee for access to premium materials, forums, webinars, and other valuable resources. Use platforms like Patreon or MemberPress to help manage your membership model effectively.

### Affiliate Marketing for Anonymous Brands

Affiliate marketing presents an effective avenue for faceless brands to monetize without the need to create their own products. By promoting third-party products and earning commissions on resulting sales, you can establish a revenue stream while remaining anonymous.

### 1. Selecting Suitable Affiliate Programs

Choose affiliate programs that resonate with your brand ethos and target audience. Endorse products or services you genuinely trust and that provide value to your followers. Popular networks include Amazon Associates, ShareASale, and Commission Junction.

### 2. Seamless Content Integration

Integrate affiliate links organically into your content—be it through blog posts, reviews, tutorials, or resource compilations. Aim for informative and helpful content rather than overtly promotional material.

### 3. Building Trust Through Transparency

Maintain transparency by disclosing your affiliate relationships. This fosters trust with your audience and ensures compliance with legal regulations. Clearly communicate that you may earn a commission from purchases made through your links.

### 4. Performance Monitoring

Utilize analytics tools to evaluate the effectiveness of your affiliate links. Track key metrics such as clicks, conversions, and overall revenue to identify successful strategies and areas for improvement.

## Sponsored Collaborations and Partnerships

Collaborating with brands for sponsored content can provide a lucrative revenue stream. Many companies are eager to pay for access to your audience and the credibility your platform offers.

### 1. Finding Compatible Partners

Identify brands that share your values and resonate with your audience. Reach out to businesses offering complementary products or services and propose mutually beneficial collaboration ideas.

### 2. Crafting Sponsored Content

Develop high-quality sponsored content that is valuable to your audience while promoting your partner's offerings. This could take the form of blog articles, social media campaigns, video content, or newsletters.

### 3. Establishing Clear Terms

Clearly define the terms of your partnership, including compensation, deliverables, timelines, and performance metrics. Make sure that both parties have a mutual understanding of their roles and duties.

### 4. Maintaining Authenticity

Keep your content genuine and pertinent to your audience's interests. Avoid promoting products that do not align with your brand or that you do not genuinely endorse, as authenticity fosters trust and builds lasting relationships.

## E-Commerce Opportunities

While digital products and affiliate marketing are excellent for faceless brands, exploring physical product sales can also be advantageous. E-commerce solutions and dropshipping allow you to sell products without managing inventory or compromising your personal information.

### 1. E-Commerce Platforms

Leverage platforms like Shopify, WooCommerce, or BigCommerce to launch an online store easily. These platforms provide the necessary tools for product management, payment processing, and shipping logistics.

### 2. Embracing Dropshipping

Consider dropshipping as a method to sell physical goods without the burden of inventory management. In this model, you market products on your site while a third-party supplier handles storage, packing, and shipping.

### 3. Custom Print-On-Demand Merchandise

Utilize print-on-demand services like Printful or Teespring to create custom-designed merchandise such as T-shirts, mugs, or posters. These services manage printing and shipping, allowing you to concentrate on design and marketing.

### 4. Creating Branded Products

Develop merchandise that resonates with your audience, including items like apparel or accessories featuring your logo or original designs.

## Consulting Services Without Revealing Your Identity

If your faceless brand is based on specialized knowledge or skills, offering consulting services can be an excellent revenue channel while preserving anonymity.

### 1. Virtual Consulting Sessions

Conduct consulting sessions via video conferencing platforms such as Zoom or Skype. Provide expert advice, strategy planning, or personalized coaching tailored to clients within your niche.

### 2. Freelance Offerings

Offer freelance expertise in areas such as writing, graphic design, web development, or marketing through platforms like Upwork, Fiverr, or Freelancer while maintaining anonymity in client interactions.

### 3. Automated Service Solutions

Create automated services—such as subscription-based resources or software tools—that deliver ongoing value without requiring continuous involvement from you.

### 4. Professional Communication Practices

Maintain professional communication channels using dedicated business accounts for client interactions to preserve anonymity while fostering trust.

## Crowdfunding as a Revenue Stream

Crowdfunding can effectively monetize your brand, particularly when creating valuable content or pursuing significant projects.

### 1. Launching Crowdfunding Campaigns

Use platforms like Kickstarter or Indiegogo to initiate crowdfunding campaigns for particular projects. Offer rewards or exclusive content as incentives for backers.

### 2. Accepting Donations

Incorporate donation options on your website or through services like PayPal or Ko-fi. Encourage audience support by emphasizing the value of their contributions.

### 3. Subscription-Based Crowdfunding Models

Combine crowdfunding efforts with subscription models through platforms like Patreon by offering tiered membership options with exclusive content and perks for subscribers.

## Advertising Revenue Strategies

Advertising can be an enduring source of income for faceless brands. By displaying ads on your website, blog, or social media channels, you can earn revenue based on views, clicks, or conversions.

### 1. Google AdSense Utilization

Enroll in Google AdSense to feature ads on your website or blog automatically matching ads relevant to your content while compensating you based on impressions or clicks.

## 2. YouTube Monetization

For video creators, joining the YouTube Partner Program allows for monetizing content through ads while adhering to YouTube's guidelines for eligibility.

## 3. Sponsored Advertising Partnerships

Collaborate with brands willing to pay for sponsored advertisements displayed on your platform or within your content while negotiating favorable terms based on audience engagement.

## 4. Implementing Native Advertising

Employ native advertising techniques to seamlessly integrate ads within your content—this often results in a less intrusive experience for viewers.

In summary, effectively monetizing a faceless brand necessitates strategic foresight and execution across various channels including digital products, affiliate marketing, sponsored partnerships, e-commerce ventures, consulting services, crowdfunding campaigns, and advertising efforts. By leveraging these strategies judiciously, you can cultivate significant revenue streams while safeguarding your anonymity. Subsequent chapters will delve deeper into additional tactics and methodologies aimed at enhancing your faceless marketing endeavors for sustained success.

# Measuring Success Through Analytics and Tracking

In the realm of marketing, particularly in faceless marketing, harnessing the power of analytics is essential for understanding performance and optimizing strategies. This chapter will explore the importance of tracking metrics, the tools available for anonymous performance analysis, and how to refine your marketing approach based on data-driven insights.

**The Significance of Analytics**

Analytics serves as a compass, guiding your marketing efforts by revealing how your audience engages with your brand. This chapter emphasizes the following key aspects of analytics:

**Deciphering Audience Behavior**: Understanding your audience's preferences and interactions with your content is vital for crafting targeted marketing campaigns that resonate effectively.

**Evaluating ROI**: By monitoring performance metrics, you can calculate the return on investment (ROI) for your marketing initiatives, allowing for more strategic resource allocation.

**Refining Strategies**: Regular insights help pinpoint successful tactics versus those needing adjustment, enabling ongoing optimization and improvement.

**Establishing Goals and KPIs**: Analytics equips you to set realistic goals and key performance indicators (KPIs), which serve as benchmarks to gauge success.

### Essential Tools for Performance Tracking

To effectively monitor and analyze your marketing performance, leveraging the right tools is crucial. Here are some indispensable resources for faceless marketing:

**Google Analytics**: A robust platform for tracking web traffic, user behavior, and conversions, providing valuable insights into visitor interactions with your site.

**Google Search Console**: Essential for monitoring your site's visibility in search results, offering data on search queries, click-through rates, and indexing issues.

**Social Media Analytics**: Each social media platform offers its own analytics tools—such as Facebook Insights and Twitter Analytics—providing crucial information on engagement and audience demographics.

**Email Marketing Analytics**: Platforms like Mailchimp and ActiveCampaign track open rates, click-through rates, and conversions from email campaigns, helping refine email strategies.

**SEO Tools**: Tools like Ahrefs and SEMrush provide insights into keyword rankings and backlink profiles, essential for evaluating SEO effectiveness.

**Heatmap Tools**: Services like Hotjar visualize user interactions on your site, revealing where visitors click, scroll, and spend their time.

### Key Metrics to Monitor

Focusing on specific metrics can help illuminate various facets of your marketing effectiveness. Key performance indicators to track include:

**Website Traffic**: Monitor the number of visitors and their sources (organic, social media, referrals).

**Bounce Rate**: Track the percentage of visitors leaving after a single page view; a high rate may indicate content or user experience issues.

**Average Session Duration**: Evaluate how long users stay on your site; longer durations suggest more engaging content.

**Pages Per Session**: Measure the average number of pages viewed per visit; more pages often reflect higher user engagement.

**Conversion Rate**: Calculate the percentage of visitors completing desired actions (purchases, sign-ups); a critical metric for assessing marketing success.

**Click-Through Rate (CTR)**: Gauge the effectiveness of calls-to-action and advertisements through the percentage of users clicking links or ads.

**Engagement Metrics**: For social media, track likes, shares, comments, and follower growth to assess content resonance.

**Open and Click Rates**: In email marketing, monitor recipient interactions to evaluate content effectiveness.

**SEO Performance**: Measure keyword rankings and organic traffic to assess SEO success.

### Setting Effective Goals and KPIs

Establishing clear goals and KPIs is vital for measuring progress. Follow these guidelines to create effective benchmarks:

**Specific**: Articulate precisely what you aim to achieve—e.g., "increase website traffic by 20% over three months."

**Measurable**: Ensure goals are quantifiable using metrics like traffic and conversion rates.

**Achievable**: Set realistic yet challenging goals based on current performance levels.

**Relevant**: Align objectives with broader business aims to ensure they contribute to your strategic vision.

**Time-Bound**: Define a clear timeframe for achieving goals to instill urgency and prioritize actions.

### Analyzing Data for Actionable Insights

Data collection is merely the beginning; analyzing that data yields actionable insights:

**Identify Trends**: Look for patterns in data to discover which content types or traffic sources yield the best results.

**Compare Across Timeframes**: Assess performance variations over different periods (month-over-month or year-over-year) to gauge growth or decline.

**Segment Your Data**: Break down data by traffic source or demographics for deeper analysis.

**Utilize Visualizations**: Employ charts and graphs to simplify data interpretation and communication of findings.

**Conduct A/B Testing**: Experiment with different variables (email subject lines, landing page designs) to determine optimal approaches.

### Commitment to Continuous Improvement

Analytics is an ongoing process; sustained success requires regular monitoring and refinement:

**Regular Reviews**: Schedule consistent assessments of performance data to stay informed about trends.

**Strategy Adjustments**: Use insights to enhance strategies; if certain content excels, consider producing more of it.

**Stay Informed**: Keep abreast of updates in analytics tools and best practices to maintain a competitive edge.

**Incorporate Feedback**: Gather audience feedback through surveys or direct inquiries to inform continuous improvement.

### Advanced Tools for Enhanced Analysis

Beyond standard analytics tools, utilizing advanced techniques can elevate your analysis:

**Advanced Analytics Platforms**: Tools like Tableau offer sophisticated data visualization capabilities for deeper insights.

**Machine Learning and AI**: Leverage AI-powered tools such as Google Cloud AI to analyze large datasets efficiently.

**Custom Dashboards**: Create tailored dashboards that consolidate key metrics from diverse sources for a holistic view of performance.

In conclusion, effective analytics and performance tracking are cornerstones of successful faceless marketing. By adopting the right tools, monitoring essential metrics, setting clear objectives, and continuously analyzing data, you can optimize your marketing efforts for significant results. The subsequent chapters will further explore advanced strategies to amplify your faceless marketing initiatives and ensure long-term success.

# Final Thoughts and Future Trends

As we conclude this exploration of faceless marketing, it's essential to reflect on the journey we've taken together. This chapter aims to distill the key insights from our discussions while also looking ahead to the future of anonymous branding. Our goal is to inspire you to embark on your own path in faceless marketing with confidence and creativity.

**Key Insights from Faceless Marketing**

Faceless marketing presents a unique opportunity for individuals and businesses to cultivate strong brands without revealing personal identities. Here are the primary takeaways that highlight its significance:

**Privacy and Security**: Maintaining anonymity can shield you from online threats, such as harassment and identity theft. It allows you to navigate the digital landscape with greater peace of mind.

**Value-Driven Focus**: This approach emphasizes the importance of content over personality. Your audience will engage with your brand based on the quality and relevance of your offerings, rather than your personal charisma.

**Scalability and Flexibility**: Without the constraints associated with a personal brand, you can easily adapt, explore new niches, and expand your reach, enabling dynamic growth for your business.

## Building a Strong Digital Presence

A successful faceless marketing strategy starts with establishing a solid digital foundation. Here are key components to consider:

**Website Optimization**: Your website acts as the central hub for your online presence. Ensure it is optimized for search engines to attract organic traffic, focusing on user experience and SEO best practices.

**Consistent Branding**: Create a cohesive brand identity that encompasses your logo, color palette, typography, and voice. Consistency fosters recognition and builds trust with your audience.

**Engaging Content**: High-quality content remains vital for audience engagement and authority building. Whether through blogs, videos, or podcasts, ensure your content aligns with your brand's mission and resonates with your target audience.

## Connecting with Your Audience

Engagement is crucial for cultivating a loyal community around your brand. Explore these avenues of connection:

**Social Media Engagement**: Use social media platforms to share valuable content, interact with followers, and promote your brand effectively. Select channels that resonate with your audience's preferences.

**Email Communication**: Build and nurture an email list to maintain direct communication with your audience. Utilize personalized and automated emails to enhance engagement and drive conversions.

**User Interaction**: Actively respond to comments, questions, and feedback. This engagement demonstrates your commitment to valuing your audience's input and strengthens the connection between you and your followers.

## Monetizing Your Faceless Brand

Consider various revenue streams to monetize your faceless brand effectively:

**Digital Products**: Develop and sell digital products such as e-books, online courses, or software that can generate substantial income while being scalable.

**Affiliate Marketing**: Partner with brands that resonate with your audience and promote their products to earn commissions on sales.

**Sponsored Collaborations**: Engage in partnerships for sponsored content that aligns with your values and provides real value to your audience.

**Consulting Services**: Offer consulting or freelance services based on your expertise while maintaining your anonymity through online platforms.

**Measuring Your Success**

To ensure continuous growth and improvement, tracking performance is essential:

**Utilize Analytics Tools**: Leverage tools like Google Analytics and social media insights to gather data on key metrics such as traffic, engagement, and conversions.

**Focus on Key Metrics**: Pay attention to metrics like bounce rates, conversion rates, click-through rates, and social media engagement to evaluate performance effectively.

**Embrace Continuous Improvement**: Regularly analyze your data to identify trends and areas for enhancement. Adapt your strategies based on insights gained to achieve better outcomes.

**Encouragement for Your Faceless Marketing Journey**

Faceless marketing transcends being merely a strategy; it embodies a philosophy centered on value, privacy, and adaptability. Here are some guiding principles as you move forward:

**Prioritize Value**: Always place value at the forefront of your offerings. Strive to meet the needs of your audience through insightful content, products, or services.

**Authenticity Matters**: Maintain transparency and honesty in all communications. Authenticity builds trust even in the absence of a personal face.

**Stay Agile**: The digital landscape is ever-changing. Be open to new technologies and trends while continuously innovating to remain competitive.

**Build Community**: Foster a sense of belonging among your audience by encouraging interactions and nurturing relationships beyond mere transactions.

By embracing these principles and implementing the strategies discussed in this guide, you can forge a successful faceless brand that capitalizes on anonymity as a strength rather than a limitation. Your journey into the world of faceless marketing awaits — dive in with enthusiasm and creativity!

www.ingramcontent.com/pod-product-compliance
Lightning Source LLC
Chambersburg PA
CBHW070419230526
45471CB00006B/2891